© Copyright 2021 - All rights reserved.

You may not reproduce, duplicate or send the contents of this book without direct written permission from the author. You cannot hereby despite any circumstance blame the publisher or hold him or her to legal responsibility for any reparation, compensations, or monetary forfeiture owing to the information included herein, either in a direct or an indirect way.

Legal Notice: This book has copyright protection. You can use the book for personal purpose. You should not sell, use, alter, distribute, quote, take excerpts or paraphrase in part or whole the material contained in this book without obtaining the permission of the author first.

Disclaimer Notice: You must take note that the information in this document is for casual reading and entertainment purposes only.
We have made every attempt to provide accurate, up to date and reliable information. We do not express or imply guarantees of any kind. The persons who read admit that the writer is not occupied in giving legal, financial, medical or other advice. We put this book content by sourcing various places.

Please consult a licensed professional before you try any techniques shown in this book. By going through this document, the book lover comes to an agreement that under no situation is the author accountable for any forfeiture, direct or indirect, which they may incur because of the use of material contained in this document, including, but not limited to, — errors, omissions, or inaccuracies.

Copyright© The Dancing Pages Publishing House
2020

BEAR

A bear's coat is made up of two unique layers: the shorter coat provides insulation from weather, while the longer coat prevents water from reaching the short coat layer and skin.

LION

A lion's roar is so powerful, that it can be heard from eight kilometres away. Also, Lion's heels don't touch the ground when it walks.

GIRAFFE

Giraffes are the tallest land animals.
A giraffe's neck alone is 1.8 meters long and weighs about 272 kilograms.
Another interesting fac about Giraffes it that Giraffes have no vocal chords.

ELEPHANT

Do you know that Elephants are th only animal that can't jump? Find else that Elephants are constantly eating, they need up to 150kg of food per day.

MONKEY

Monkeys can understand written numbers and can even count. They can also understand basic parts of arithmetic and even, in rare cases, multiplication.

PELICAN

Along with the giant pouch, pelicans are a large bird with short legs, and they appear rather clumsy on land.
Once in the water, they are strong swimmers, thanks to their webbed feet.

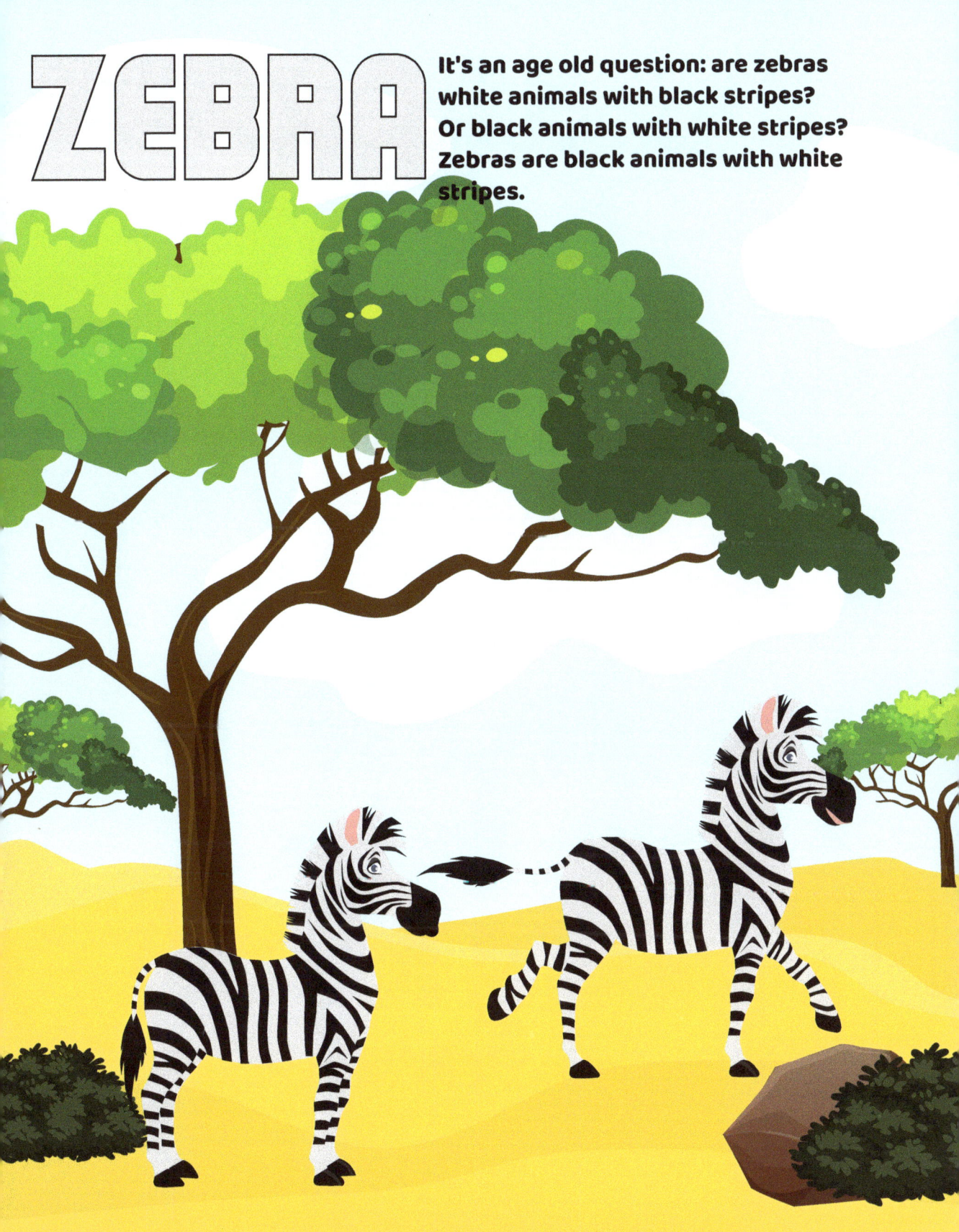

RHINOCEROS

A rhinoceros horn is made of hair.
Also Rhinos love rolling in mud, but they do this for protection.
Mud Coat protect Rinos from insects bitting and keep them cool.

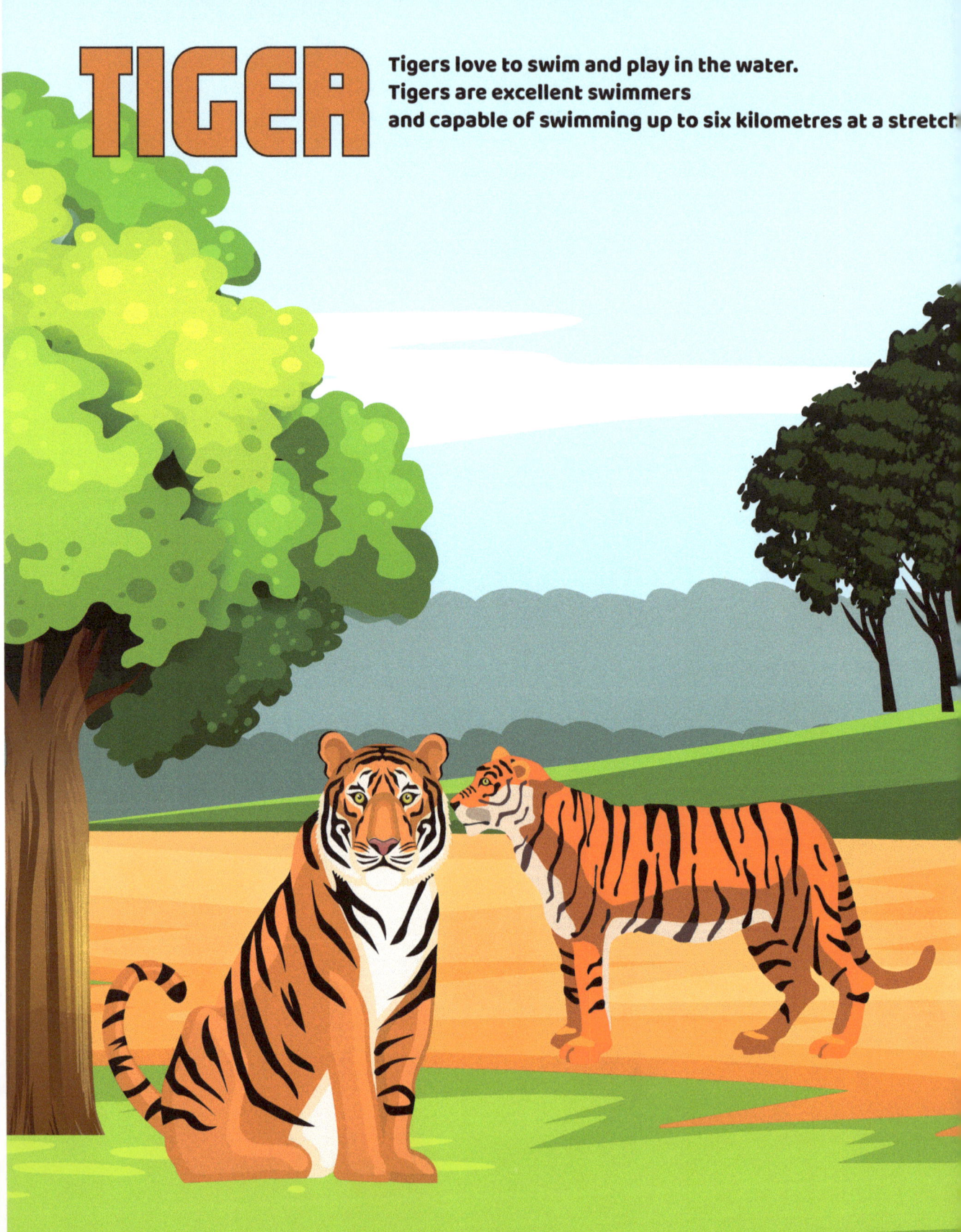

ANTELOPE

Antelope are smart! They follow the rains to find tender grasses. They also often follow zebras because they eat the tougher, outer grass leaving the soft,

WOLF

Wolves are extremely timid and shy, they don't chase or hunt people, and tend to want to get away from humans as soon as they catch our smell.

ALLIGATOR

Alligators have between 74 and 80 teeth in their mouth. They continue to grow throughout their lifetimes.

HIPPOPOTAMUS

Hippos spend pretty much their whole lives in the water, but they cannot swim.
They can eat more than 40 kilograms of grass in one night.
Hippos are most active at night.

PEACOCK

The large colorful "tail" which they have become known for, is actually called a "train". Peacock feathers are covered in tiny crystals.

FOX

Foxes are solitary and they live in underground dens. What does the fox say? As it turns out, foxes can produce a variety of sounds — up to 40 to be exact.

FLAMINGO

The word "flamingo" comes from the Spanish and Latin word "flamenco," which means fire. Flamingos hold their bent bills upside down while feeding.

MEERKAT

Meerkats are known to use a wide range of vocal calls to communicate between one another sounding long howls to warn the rest of the band of an approaching bird of prey, and using short double-barks to alert them of a predator nearing the group on the ground.

IGUANA

They've got excellent eyesight allowing them to spot prey or detect danger a long way away. Although classed as omnivores they tend to stick to an herbivorous diet

THANK YOU.

We hope you enjoyed our book.
As a small family company, your feedback is very important to us.
Please let us know how you like our book at:

the.dancing.pages@gmail.com

www.ingramcontent.com/pod-product-compliance
Lightning Source LLC
LaVergne TN
LVHW070211080526
838202LV00063B/6588